I want to be a
GYMNAST

By Eugene Baker

Illustrated by Lois Axeman

 CHILDRENS PRESS, CHICAGO

Library of Congress Cataloging in Publication Data

Baker, Eugene H
 I want to be a gymnast.

 SUMMARY: A young girl and her classmates learn about
the basic skills required of a gymnast.
 1. Gymnastics—Juvenile literature. [1. Gymnastics.
2. Occupations] I. Axeman, Lois. II. Title.
GV511.B34   796.4'1   75-35502
ISBN 0-516-01733-0

Amy called to her friends down the hall. "Look at this!"

A neat sign hung next to the gym. SPECIAL GYMNASTICS SHOW NEXT FRIDAY AT THE HIGH SCHOOL. SIGN UP BELOW. SEE MRS. ANDREWS FOR TICKETS.

Amy reached for her pencil, "Let's sign up, everyone."

Kathleen nodded her head, "We can get our permission slips right after school."

Just then Mrs. Andrews came through the door. "Hi, glad to see you are interested in gymnastics. We will start our own unit in gym class next week."

The following Friday the students from Thomas School went to the high school. The gym was already set up for the show.

"This is the equipment they use," explained Mrs. Andrews.

"The men work on six different events—floor exercise, pommel horse, parallel bars, the horizontal bars, vaulting, and the rings."

"There are four different gymnastic events for women. They are floor exercise, balance

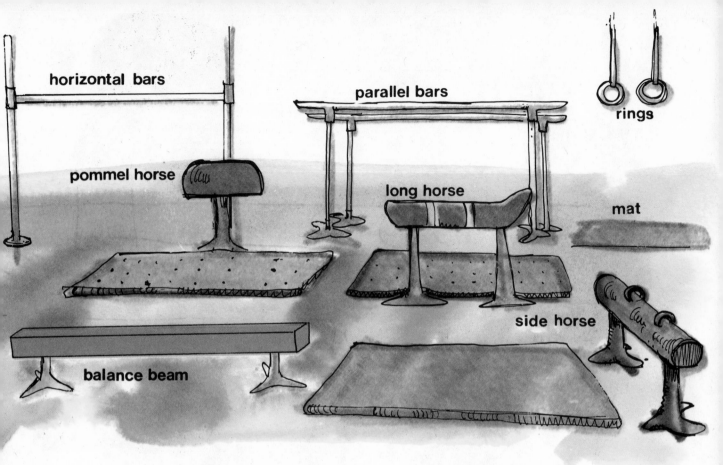

horizontal bars

parallel bars

rings

pommel horse

long horse

mat

side horse

balance beam

beam, the uneven parallel bars, and vaulting."

"The trampoline event is in many high school programs. In college, however, trampolining is a separate sport," Mrs. Andrews said.

After the show, Mrs. Andrews
asked, "What do you think
about gymnastics now?"

"It's great," Larry answered. "You do not have to be big or very tall to be a good gymnast."

Amy smiled, "I liked the floor exercise. Everyone did the same things. But they did different things, too."

"I liked the way the men worked on the rings," Steve said.

"I liked the uneven parallel bars best," Robyn added.

"A gymnast must do all those different things well," Mrs. Andrews answered. "A good gymnast must be a good athlete."

Next Monday in gym class Mrs. Andrews said, "Today we begin gymnastics. We will not need special equipment. We will work on tumbling mats. First we will learn the twelve basic gymnastic skills."

"We will have Parents' Night
at the end of this unit. Some
students will show their
gymnastic skills then."

Amy whispered to Kathleen
and Robyn "Let's help each
other. I would like to be in that
program."

"Me too," nodded Kathleen.

"Remember," said Mrs. Andrews, "you must do well with each exercise. Then you may go on to the next one. After you know these twelve basic skills, you will learn to do them on equipment."

"OK everyone, let's begin." Mrs. Andrews moved to the tumbling mat.

"Our first movement is the Front Tuck Roll. Bend your

knees like this. Place your
hands on the mat in front of you.
Then straighten your legs and
push your body forward." Mrs.
Andrews made a Front Tuck
Roll.

13

The students began to practice. Mrs. Andrews moved from mat to mat checking.

"Our second movement is the Back Tuck Roll. It is like the forward roll, but this time you roll backwards."

Mrs. Andrews pointed to Amy. "Amy, do a Back Tuck Roll, please. Remember, rolling

backwards needs more push
with your arms."

Amy pushed hard and rolled
back. Mrs. Andrews smiled.

"Very good. Staying in that small ball as you roll over is called the tuck position."

Throughout the next few weeks, the boys and girls practiced.

"Movement number three is the Back Straddle Roll," said Mrs. Andrews. "This is the same

as the tuck roll except your legs
are spread apart."

"The fourth movement is the
Front Straddle Roll. It looks like
this."

"Our fifth movement is one you all know—the Head Balance. Some people have problems with this one. Please put your head far in front of your hands. Press with your hands. Form a triangle with your head and each hand. The secret is to keep your weight evenly balanced between all three points."

"Our sixth movement is the Front Scale. This is a very basic movement in gymnastics. Balance correctly on one foot."

"Next is the Handstand. This is movement number seven. It

will take time to learn this. Lean
forward with the shoulders,
keep your head up. Now, kick to
a handstand keeping one leg in
front of the other."

"Next we have the Cartwheel. Think of a straight line on the ground. Stand at one end of the line. Kick your leg forward and up while turning your body to the right. Keep your legs wide apart. OK everyone, let's try it."

One day Mrs. Andrews said,
"These last four exercises are
the hardest. Number nine is the
Back Extension Roll. Number

ten and eleven are the Front
Limber and the Back Limber.
Number twelve, the last one, is
the Front Headspring."

"To help you learn these
exercises I asked the older
gymnasts to work with groups
of four."

Two weeks later, Mrs. Andrews said, "You have all done very well. It takes time to learn gymnastic skills. I would like the following students to report to me after school for special practice. These people will be in the Parents' Night program: Julie, Larry, Bob, Jane, Amy, Robyn, Steve, Kathleen, and Scott.

On the night of the program,
each student performed. Each
routine included combinations
of the basic movements.

The program was a great
success. Amy's mother and
father congratulated her.

"You were great," Dad said.

"You looked beautiful," added Mother.

"Thank you," smiled Amy. "I'm going to keep practicing. I want to be a good gymnast."

Amy picked up her shoes and looked around. "You know, Dad, some day I may even be in the Olympics."

"Why not!" smiled Dad. "Maybe you will be the one to win a gold medal for the United States."

About the Author:

Dr. Baker was graduated from Carthage College, Carthage, Illinois. He got his master's degree and doctorate in education at Northwestern University. He has worked as a teacher, as a principal, and as a director of curriculum and instruction. Now he works full time as a curriculum consultant. His practical help to schools where new programs are evolving is sparked with his boundless enthusiasm. He likes to see social studies and language arts taught with countless resources and many books to encourage students to think independently, creatively, and critically. The Bakers, who live in Arlington Heights, Illinois, have a son and two daughters.

About the Artist:

Lois Axeman is a native Chicagoan who lives with her husband and two children in the city. After attending the American Academy and the Institute of Design (IIT), Lois started as a fashion illustrator in a department store. When the childrens wear illustrator became ill, Lois took her place and found she loved drawing children. She started free-lancing then, and has been doing text and picture books ever since.